What Do TEACHERS Do?

Rita Kidde

PowerKiDS press
New York

For my mother, who is a dedicated, creative, and nurturing teacher
A mi madre, que es una maestra dedicada, bondadosa y creativa

Published in 2015 by The Rosen Publishing Group, Inc.
29 East 21st Street, New York, NY 10010

First Edition

Editor: Amelie von Zumbusch
Book Design: Colleen Bialecki
Photo Research: Katie Stryker

Photo Credits: Cover Fuse/Getty Images; p. 5 Brand X Pictures/Stockbyte/Thinkstock; p. 6 Steve Debenport/E+/Getty Images; p. 9 Digital Vision/Photodisc/Thinkstock; pp. 10, 14, 18 Comstock Images/Stockbyte/Thinkstock; p. 13 JupiterImages/ Stockbyte/Thinkstock; p. 17 David Buffington/Blend Images/Thinkstock; p. 21 LWA/Taxi/Getty Images; p. 22 XiXinXing/ Thinkstock; p. 24 Cynthia Farmer/Shutterstock.com.

Publisher's Cataloging Data

Kidde, Rita.
What do teachers do? / by Rita Kidde. — 1st ed.
        p. cm. — (Jobs in my school)
Includes an index.
ISBN: 978-1-4777- 6556-2 (Library Binding)
ISBN: 978-1-4777- 6559-3 (Paperback)s
ISBN: 978-1-4777- 6560-9 (6-pack)
1. Teachers—Juvenile literature. 2. Teachers.   I. Title.
LB1775.K57 2015
371.2

Manufactured in the United States of America

CPSIA Compliance Information: Batch #WS14PK4: For Further Information contact Rosen Publishing, New York, New York at 1-800-237-9932

CONTENTS

Teachers work in **schools**.
They help kids learn.

They can make school fun!

Teachers know a lot. They work hard, too.

The United States has more than three million teachers!

Massachusetts had the first public school.

Texas has the most teachers.

Teachers' Day is May 7.

Most schools have
many teachers.

19

There are **art** teachers, gym teachers, and music teachers.

21

How many teachers do
you know?

WORDS TO KNOW

art

school

teacher

WEBSITES

Due to the changing nature of Internet links, PowerKids Press has developed an online list of websites related to the subject of this book. This site is updated regularly. Please use this link to access the list: www.powerkidslinks.com/josc/teach/

INDEX